How to Draw Zentangle® Art

DRAWING ZENTANGLE® HOLIDAYS

Hannah Geddes

Gareth Stevens
PUBLISHING

Acknowledgments

The Zentangle® method was created by Rick Roberts and Maria Thomas.

"Zentangle"®, the Zentangle logo, "Anything is possible one stroke at a time", "Bijou", "Certified Zentangle Teacher"®, "CZT"®, "Zentangle Apprentice"®, and "Zentomology" are trademarks, service marks, or certification marks of Rick Roberts, Maria Thomas, and/or Zentangle Inc.

All the tangles in this book are Zentangle® originals created by Rick Roberts and Maria Thomas, apart from: Aztec (page 15) by Hannah Geddes CZT.

Please visit our website, www.garethstevens.com.
For a free color catalog of all our high-quality books,
call toll free 1-800-542-2595 or fax 1-877-542-2596.

CATALOGING-IN-PUBLICATION DATA

Names: Geddes, Hannah.
Title: Drawing Zentangle® holidays / Hannah Geddes.
Description: New York : Gareth Stevens Publishing, 2018. | Series: How to draw Zentangle® art | Includes index.
Identifiers: ISBN 9781538207222 (pbk.) | ISBN 9781538207185 (library bound) | ISBN 9781538207093 (6 pack)
Subjects: LCSH: Drawing--Technique--Juvenile literature. | Repetitive patterns (Decorative arts)--Juvenile literature. | Holiday decorations in art--Juvenile literature.
Classification: LCC NC730.G43 2018 | DDC 741.201'9--dc23

Published in 2018 by
Gareth Stevens Publishing
111 East 14th Street, Suite 349
New York, NY 10003

Step-outs and Zentangle® Inspired Artworks by Hannah Geddes
Text by Catherine Ard
Outline illustrations by Katy Jackson
Designed by Trudi Webb and Emma Randall
Edited by Frances Evans

Printed in China

CPSIA compliance information: Batch CS17GS: For further information contact Gareth Stevens, New York, New York at 1-800-542-2595.

Contents

Getting Festive

Zentangle® is a drawing method created by Rick Roberts and Maria Thomas. It teaches you how to create beautiful pieces of art using simple **patterns** called tangles. Tangling is a really fun, relaxing way to get creative, and it brings out the artist in everyone. You can tangle wherever and whenever the mood takes you!

Holidays and festivals bring out the creativity in everyone. You can decorate your home, create your own cards, and even make artwork to give as gifts. This book will teach you how to create Zentangle® Inspired Artworks ("ZIAs") based on four festive celebrations. Each project has tangles that suit its theme, but you can also mix and match any tangles you want!

amazon.com

Remit To:

Amazon.com
PO Box 80367
Seattle, WA 98108-80387
USA

SDRhJdXdJR

Vendor Return
Shipment ID: 36575058572551
VRET ID: VRET7641100096531
Process Date: May 9, 2026
IOG: Amazon.com

Shipped From:
4000 Premier Parkway
SAINT PETERS , MO 63376-3447
United States

Shipping Address
Gareth Stevens Publishing
BETHANY FULFILLMENT WAREHOUSE
802 N 41ST ST
BETHANY, MO 64424-7201
United States

Amazon.com Vendor Return -- OVERSTOCK

Qty.	Item	ASIN	UPC/EAN
	SINGLE-PACKAGE SHIPMENT		
1	Drawing Zentangle Holidays (How to Draw Zentangle Art)	1538207222	9781538207222

0/DRhJdXdJR/-1 of 1-//STL5-NIT/vendor-returns/0/0516-13:45/0515-08:19 Pack Type : Smartpac
VRET36575058572551

Pens and Pencils

Pencils are good for drawing "strings" (page 18) and for adding shade to your tangles. A 01 (0.25-mm) black pen is good for fine lines. Use a 05 (0.45-mm) or 08 (0.50-mm) pen to fill in bigger areas. You can use paints to brighten up your art, too!

Paper

Tangles are usually drawn on a square 3.5-inch (9 cm) tile made of thin cardboard. You can use any kind of paper, but if you want to make your tangles really special, use good quality art paper. Have some tracing paper on hand so you can trace the images in this book to use as outlines for your Zentangle® Inspired Artworks.

Useful Techniques

There are some special techniques you might come across when you tangle. A "highlight" is a gap or blank space in the lines of your tangles. Highlights can make your tangles look shiny!

An "aura" is a line traced around the inside or outside of a shape. Use auras to add a sense of movement to your art.

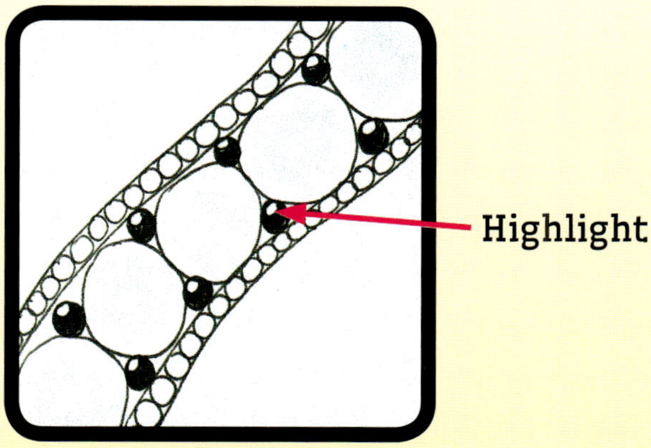

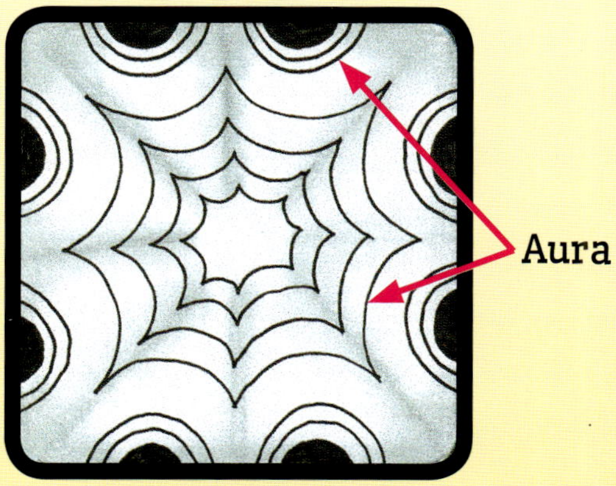

Essential Tangles

Here are some fantastic tangles to get you started! You can practice drawing each tangle on a square tile (see step 1 on page 18 for instructions). Each project in this book has a tangle key that tells you where to find the instructions for the tangles that have been used.

Tipple

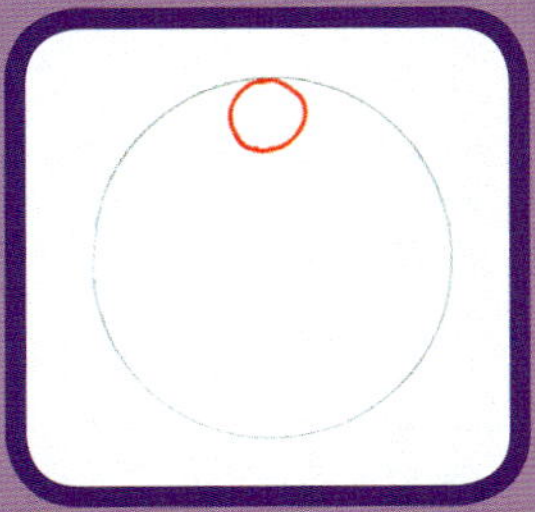

1. Start by drawing a small circle on your paper.

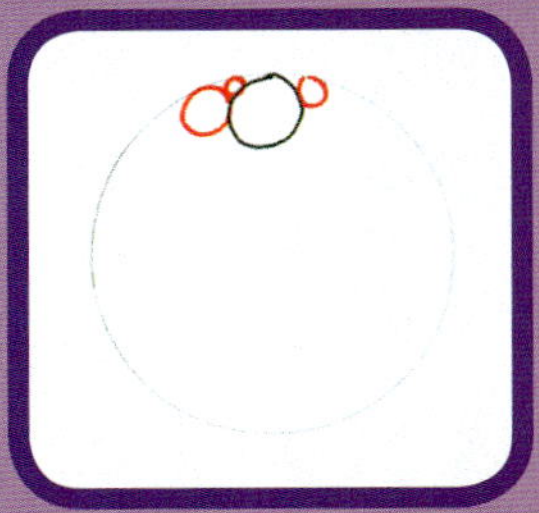

2. Add a few more circles around the first one. They can be any size you like.

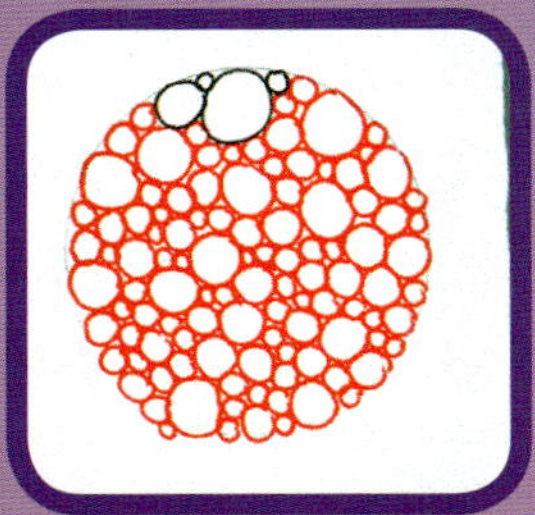

3. Keep drawing circles of different sizes until the chosen space is full.

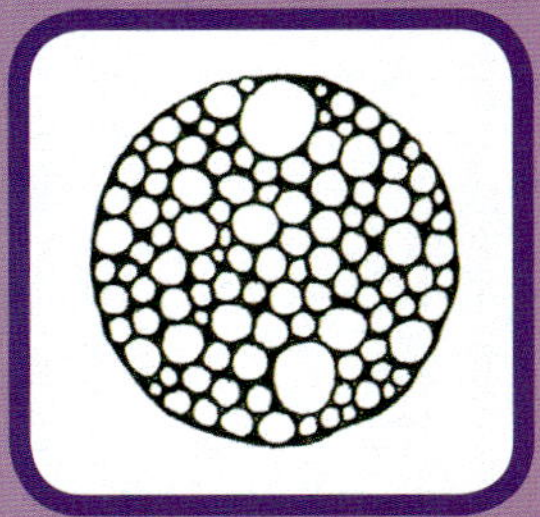

4. Shade in the spaces between the circles to finish your tangle.

Bales

1. Draw evenly-spaced **diagonal** lines across the paper.

2. Draw diagonal lines in the opposite direction to make a **grid**.

3. Draw bumps along the bottom of all of the lines you drew in step 1.

4. Then draw bumps along the top of these lines.

5. Repeat steps 3 and 4 on the diagonal lines that you drew in step 2.

6. Your pretty tangle is finished.

Keeko

1. Draw four **horizontal** lines next to each other. They should be the same length and equally spaced apart.

2. Draw another four lines next to the first set, but this time make the lines **vertical**.

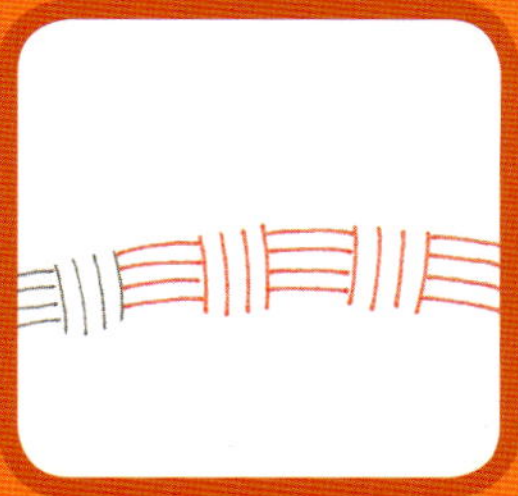

3. Repeat steps 1 and 2 until the row is complete.

4. Underneath each set of four horizontal lines, draw a set of four vertical lines.

5. Draw a set of four horizontal lines underneath each set of vertical lines.

6. Fill the chosen area, and then add some shading to finish it.

Cadent

1. Draw a grid made up of small circles.

2. Draw a curve from the top of the first circle to the bottom of the second circle.

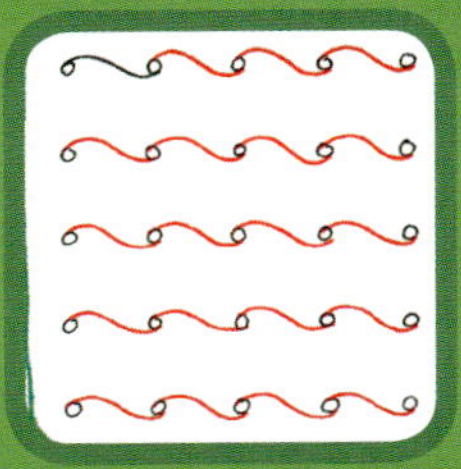

3. Repeat this pattern across each horizontal row of circles.

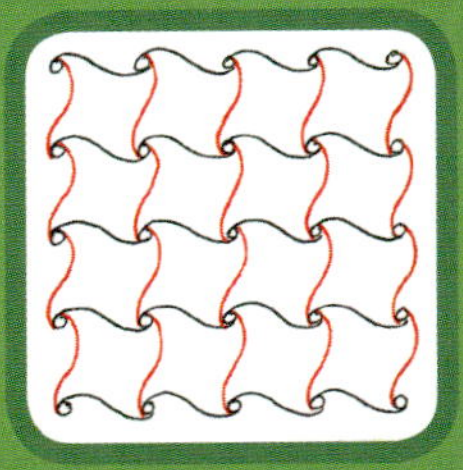

4. Now, use the same pattern to join up the vertical lines of circles.

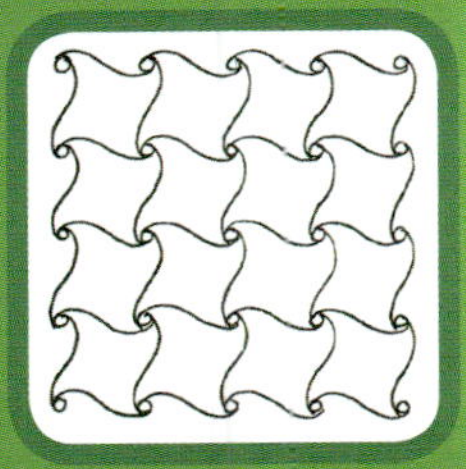

5. Your Cadent tangle is complete.

'Nzeppel

1. Draw horizontal and vertical lines over the paper to make a grid.

2. Now draw diagonal lines in both directions over the paper. They should be evenly spaced so they run through the middle of each square in the grid.

3. Each square in the grid should now be split into four triangular sections. Draw around the shape of each triangle, but round off the corners to create this pebble-like effect.

4. Continue to fill each square with triangles, as shown.

5. Add some shading to finish your tangle.

Printemps

This tangle is perfect for creating swirly textures.

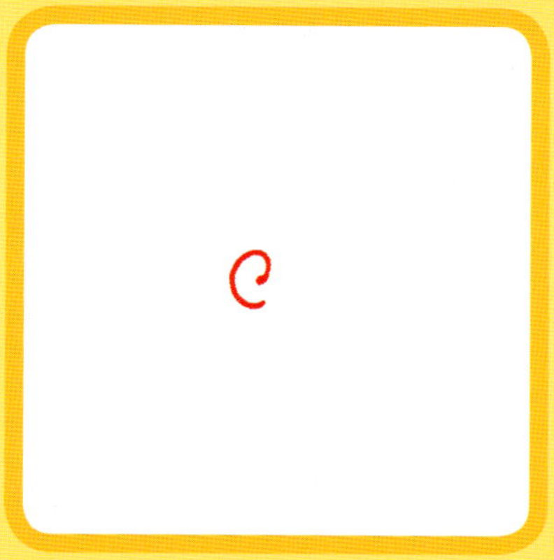

1. Draw a dot in the middle of your page. Then begin to draw a small spiral starting from the dot.

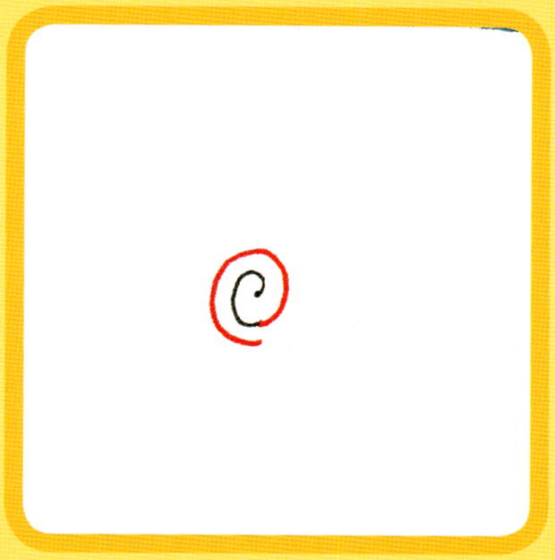

2. Continue drawing your spiral. You can make it as small or as big as you like.

3. Once the spiral is the size that you want, turn the line in to close up the shape. You should have a smooth circle around the edge.

4. Add more spiral shapes around the first one.

5. Continue drawing Printemps spirals until you have filled the space.

AHH

This flashy tangle adds a burst of festivity to any holiday picture.

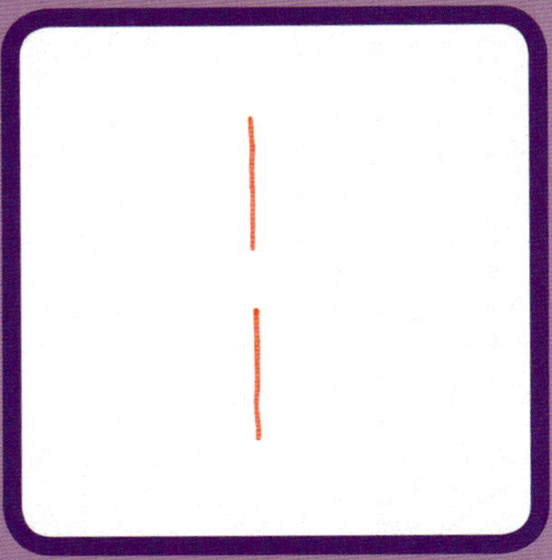

1. Draw two vertical lines, leaving a gap in the middle.

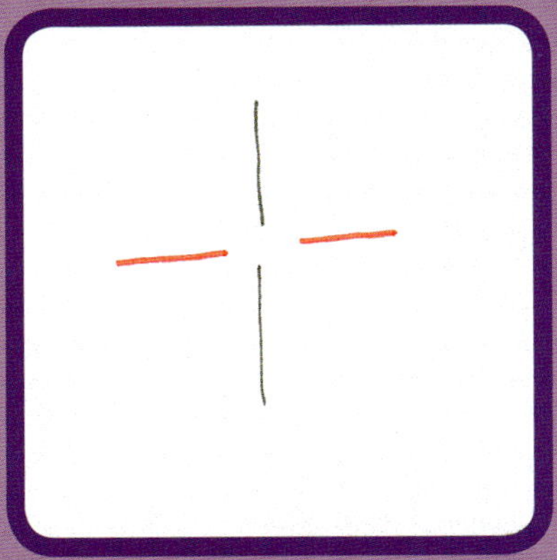

2. Draw two horizontal lines to make a cross shape, still leaving a small gap in the middle.

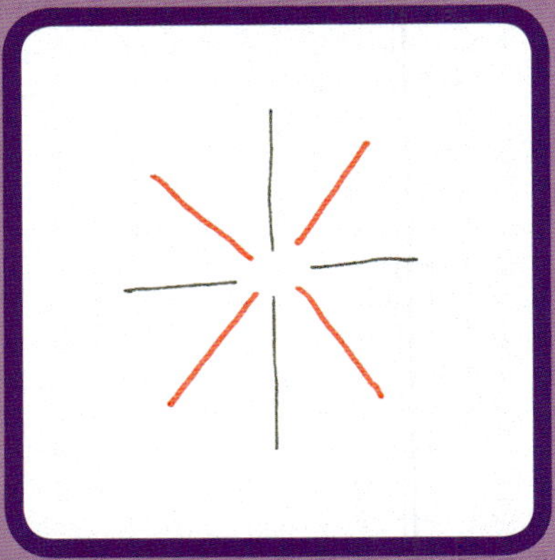

3. Add four more lines in an "X" shape, leaving a gap in the middle.

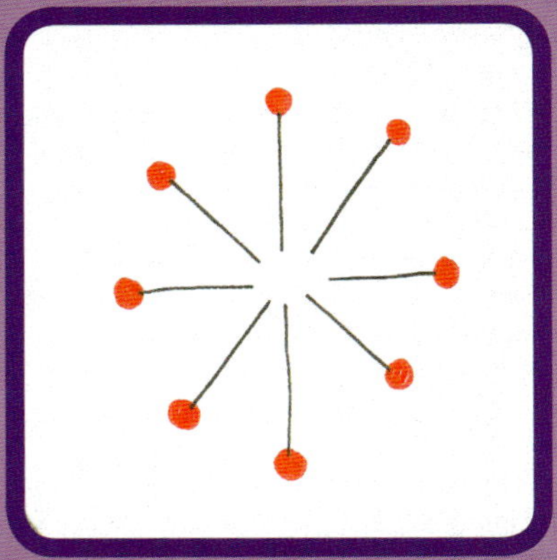

4. Add a circle at the end of each line and use your pen to fill them in.

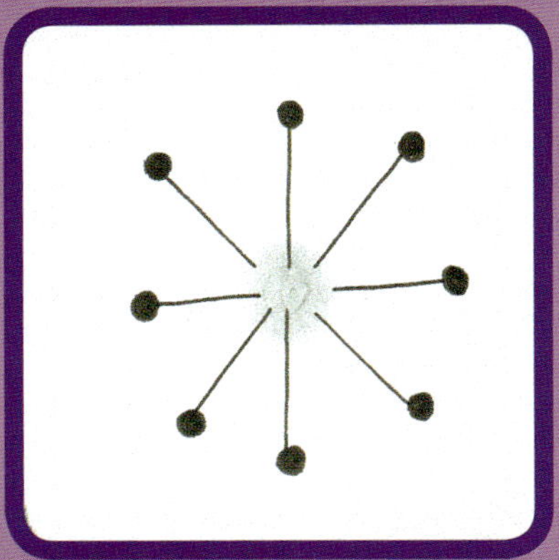

5. Add a smudge of pencil to the gap in the middle.

Tangle Tip!
The smudge in the middle of AHH really adds some twinkle. This tangle would look great on a homemade Christmas card!

Stoic

Wrap this **woven** tangle around any shape for a bold basket effect.

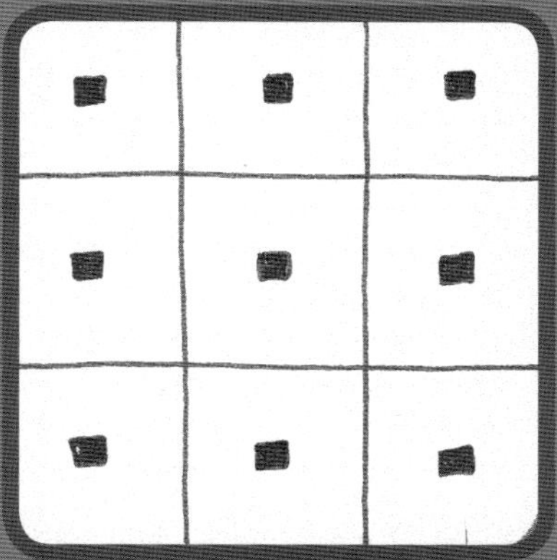

1. Divide the paper into a grid of squares by drawing vertical and horizontal lines. Draw a small square in the middle of each square and fill it in with your pen.

2. Draw a line from the top edge of every small square to meet the line on the right.

3. Now draw a line from the right edge of every small square to meet the line below.

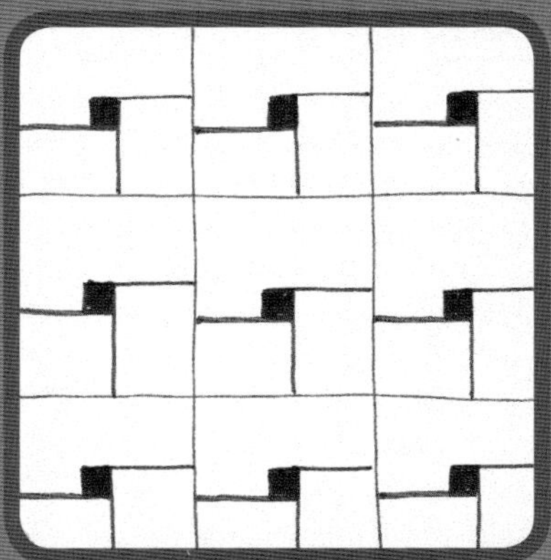

4. Continue by drawing a line from the bottom edge of every small square to meet the line on the left.

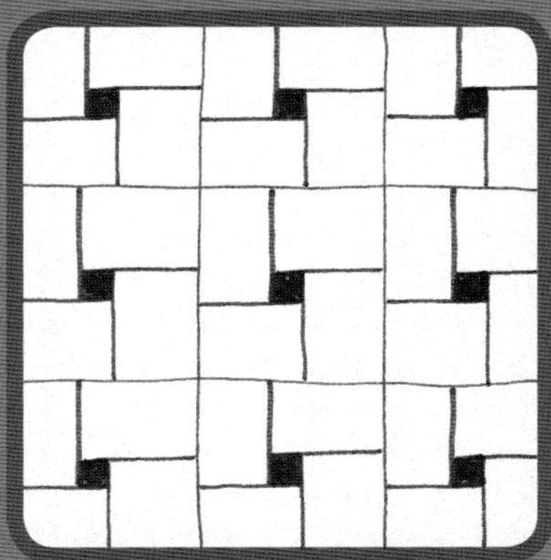

5. Finish the tangle by drawing a line from the left edge of every small square to meet the line above.

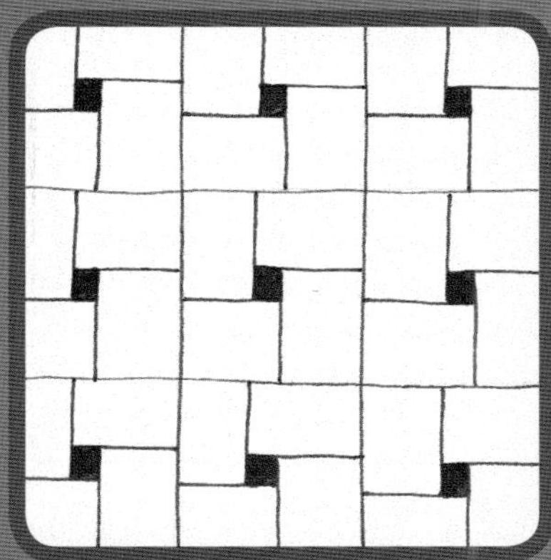

6. Your pretty tangle is complete!

Eye-wa

Look at this eye-popping pattern for long enough and you might see it staring back at you!

1. Start by drawing vertical and horizontal lines over the paper to make a grid.

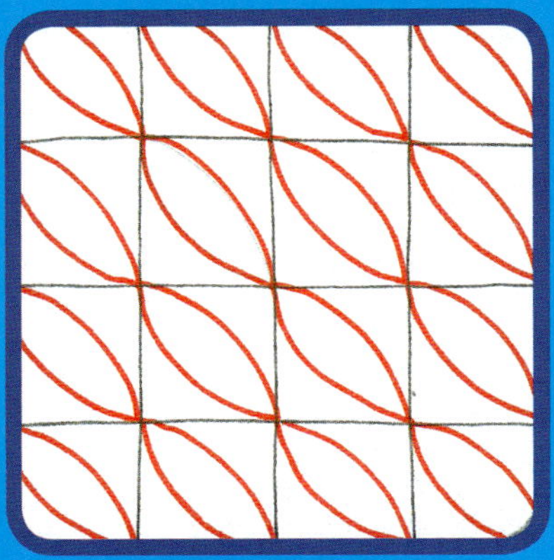

2. In each square, draw a pointed petal shape from top left to bottom right.

3. Use your pen to fill in the spaces on either side of the petal shapes in every other square.

4. Now fill in the petal shape in every square that has not been shaded.

5. Your dizzy tangle is finished!

Eke

This twirly tangle looks like pretty party streamers or strings of festive fairy lights.

1. Start by drawing a loop that looks like an "e" with a long tail.

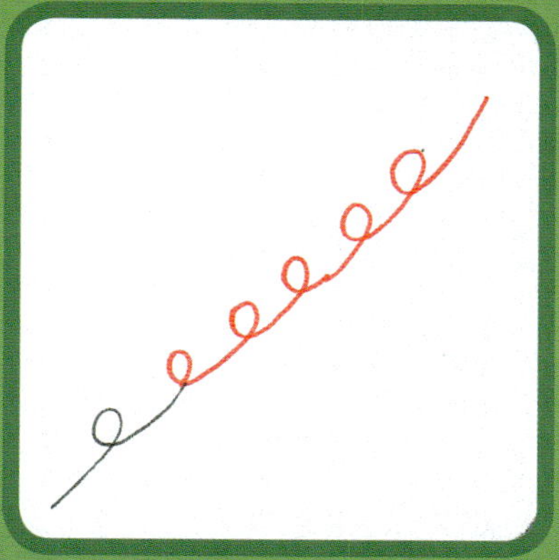

2. Repeat with a long row of joined up loops.

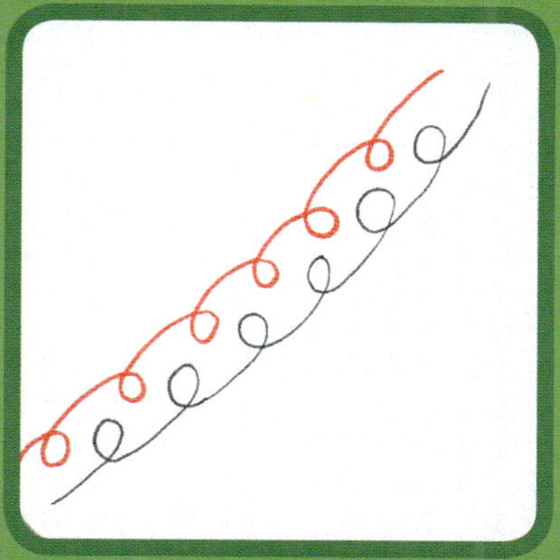

3. Now draw a row of upside-down loops opposite the first row. Make the circles in these loops sit in the spaces between the loops opposite.

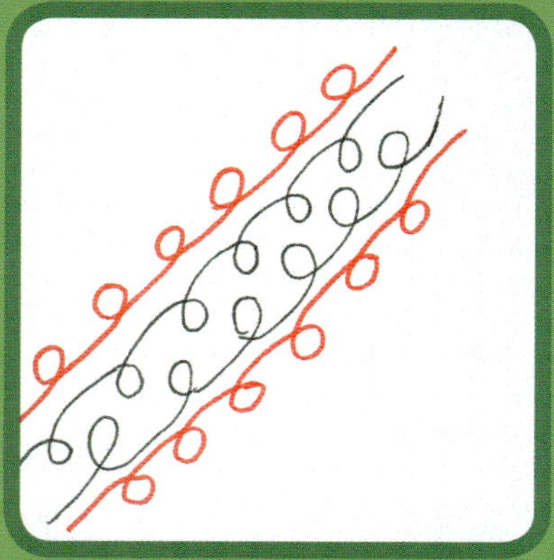

4. Repeat with rows of loops on either side, alternating the way the loops face each time.

5. Continue adding loops until you have filled the space. Add some shading and smudge to finish.

Tangle Tip!

Eye-wa and Eke are good tangles to use to fill up a large space. You could draw them onto plain wrapping paper to give your presents a personal touch!

Stricles

This bendy, spotty tangle will knock your socks off!

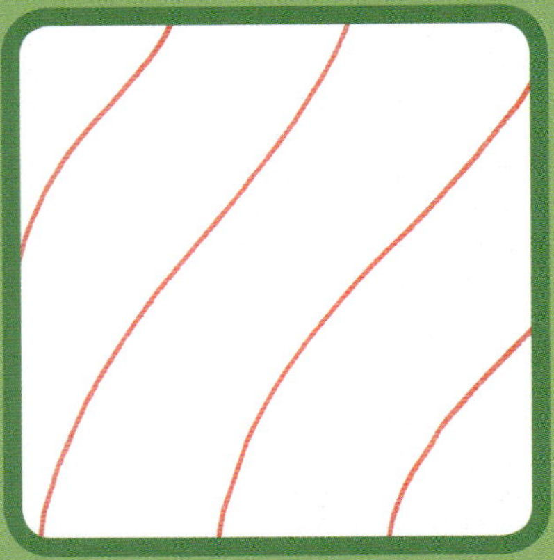

1. Draw wavy lines at an angle across the paper.

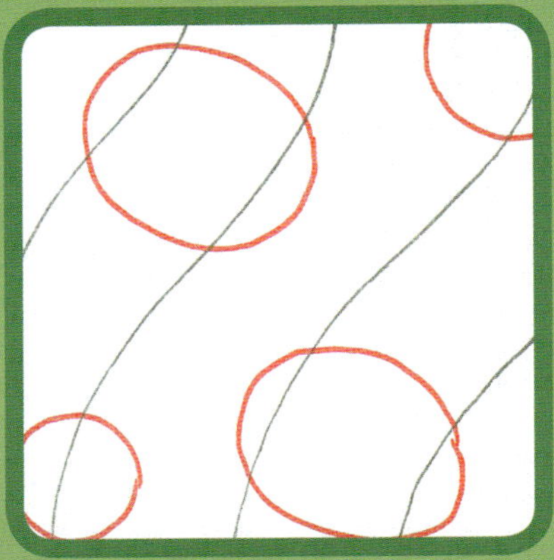

2. Add big circles overlapping one or two of the wavy lines.

3. Using your pen, shade between every other pair of lines to make stripes. Don't shade inside the circles.

4. Now fill in the part of each circle that does not overlap one of the shaded stripes.

5. Your tangle is finished!

Aztec

Use this tangle as a border around the edge of an outline, or to neatly fill a narrow space.

1. Draw a shape like an "S" with straight lines instead of curves.

2. Add a straight line at either end of your "S" shape.

3. Add a row of these shapes and draw two straight lines above and below the row.

4. Your tangle is complete!

Tangle Tip!

You don't have to add the band of lines above the shapes. Check out the Aztec tangle on the angel! (pages 22-23).

Beeline

Use Beeline to give a flat surface a blocky 3-D look.

1. Begin by drawing evenly-spaced horizontal lines across the page.

2. Starting in the top left, draw a vertical zigzag line down the page. Each point in the zigzag must meet a horizontal line.

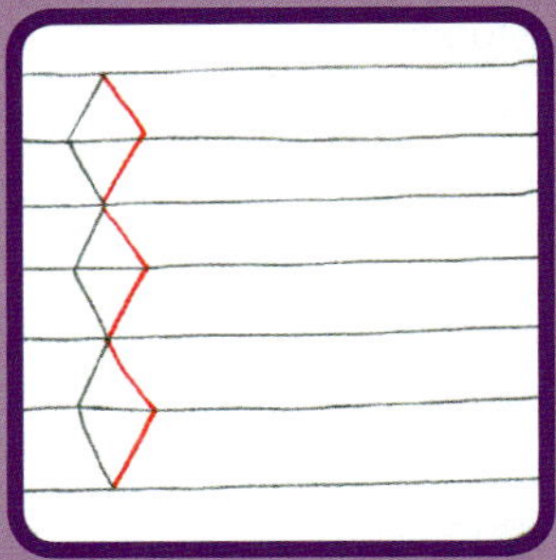

3. Now draw a zigzag line opposite the first one to form a row of diamonds.

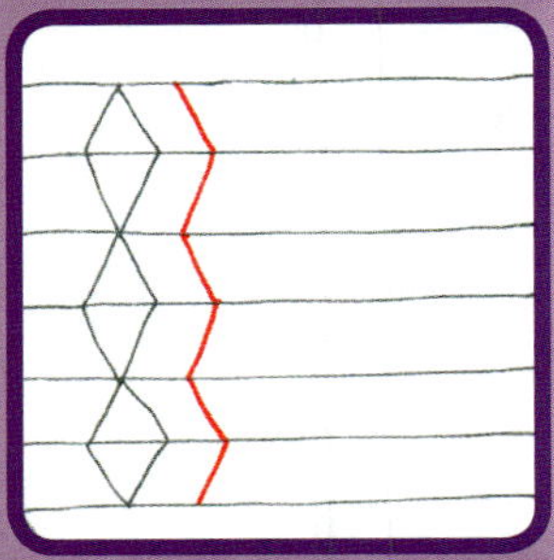

4. Draw another zigzag following the outline of the previous row.

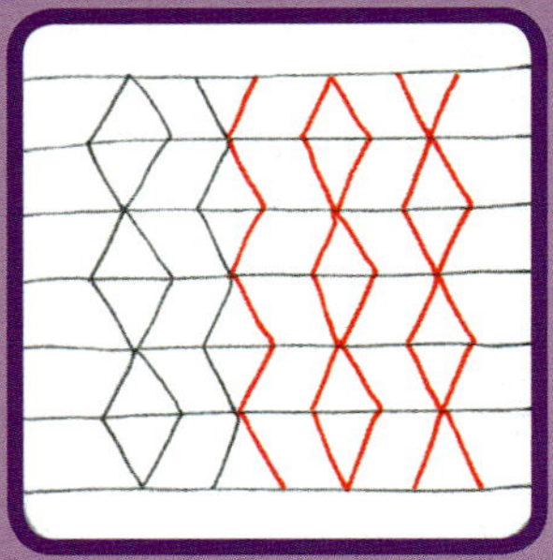

5. Repeat steps 2 to 4 until the area is filled with rows of diamonds.

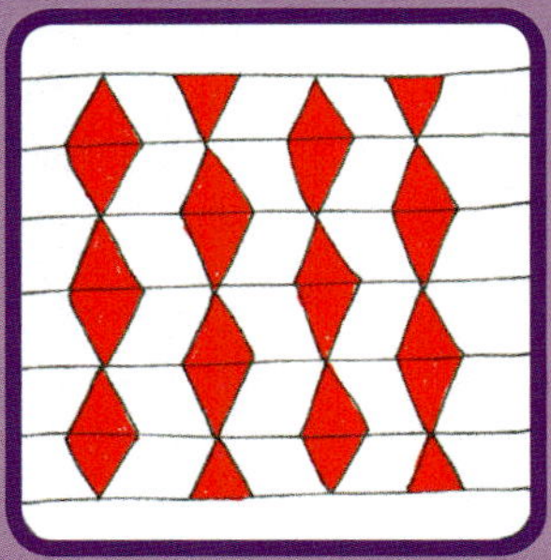

6. Fill in all of the triangle and diamond shapes with your pen.

7. Shade between the horizontal lines in every other row to finish the tangle.

Chillon

The soft waves and cushioning curves of this relaxed tangle make it really easy on the eye.

1. Draw evenly spaced diagonal lines across the paper.

2. Draw diagonal lines in the opposite direction to make a grid of squares.

3. Draw bumps along the tops of all the diagonal lines going one way. Each bump should start and end at the corner of a square.

4. To finish, draw bumps along the tops of the diagonal lines going in the other direction.

5. Your pretty, bumpy tangle is ready!

Tangle Tip!

You could add extra detail where the lines cross, to vary the look. Have a look at how we've used Chillon on page 27!

Strings, Tangles, and ZIAs

The Zentangle® method begins with drawing "strings." These are pencil lines that separate spaces inside a shape. The spaces are then filled with tangles to create your ZIA. Each project in this book starts with an outline of a festive object with the strings already drawn in.

These steps show you how to build up a set of Zentangle® patterns on a Zentangle® tile. Tiles are good for practicing the tangles you've just learned. They can also be works of art themselves!

1. To create a square tile, use a ruler and pencil to draw four evenly-spaced dots for the corners. Connect the dots with straight lines.

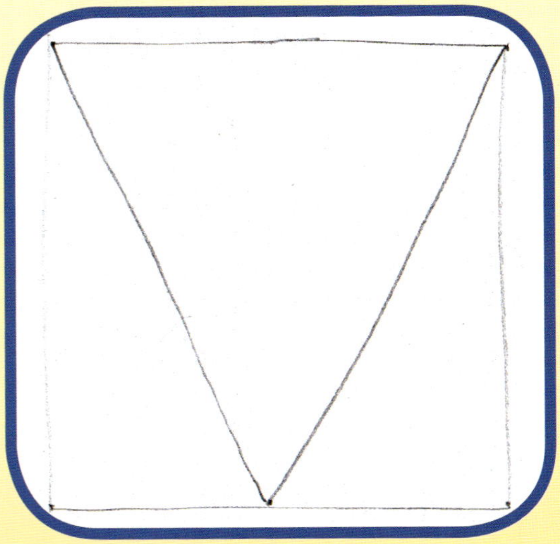

2. Now add strings to divide up the square. Draw a dot in the center of the bottom line. Then draw strings from the top corners to the new dot. This will create three triangle shapes to fill with tangles.

3. Choose a section to fill and a tangle to start with. We've chosen Printemps (page 9). Starting in one corner and using a pen, carefully fill the area with the tangle.

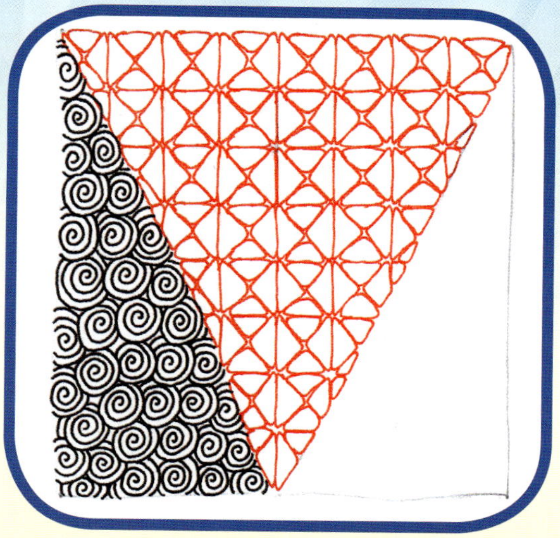

4. Now move to the next space created by the string. We've chosen to fill this section with 'Nzeppel (page 8).

5. In the final space, we've used Bales (page 7).

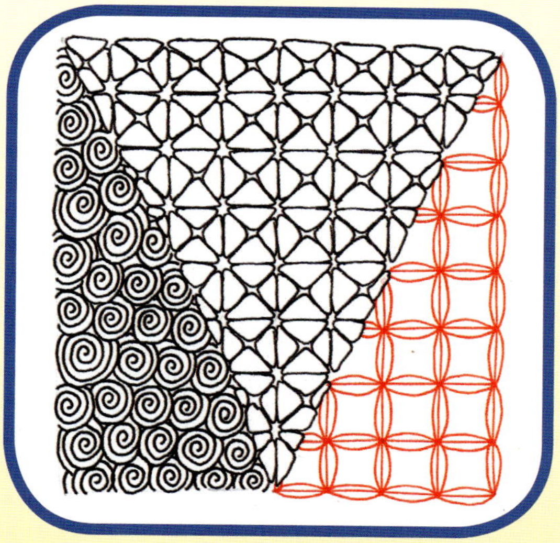

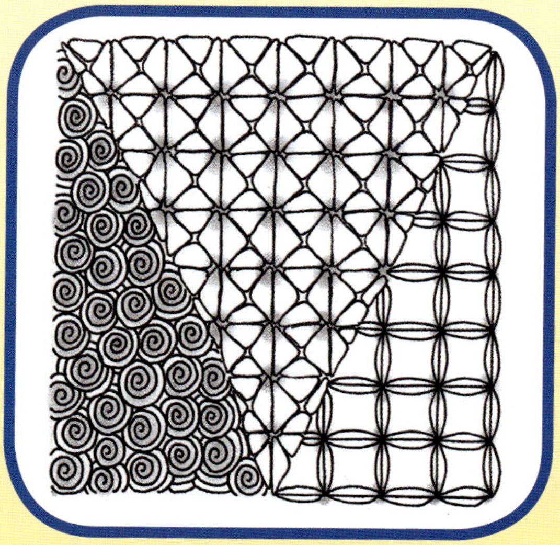

6. To complete the tangles, add shading to create shape and texture.

Now you're ready to start your own tangles!

Christmas Tree

You can get into the Christmas spirit any time of year! Draw this fine pine, hang festive tangles on its branches, and top it off with a sparkling star.

1. Draw or trace the outline of a Christmas tree with layers of branches.

2. Start to add some tangles. We've used a single spiral from Printemps to make pretty ornaments and we're filling in the tree with AHH.

TANGLE KEY

AHH: page 10
'Nzeppel : page 8
Printemps: page 9
Stoic: page 11

3. This version of Stoic gives the basket underneath the tree a nice woven effect.

4. We've used a single flower of 'Nzeppel in the center of the star. We added some lines on each point to create a 3-D look.

Peaceful Angel

Angels are symbols of peace and goodwill at Christmas time. Follow these steps to create your own beautiful angel with wonderfully tangled wings.

1. Draw or trace the outline of an angel. Add strings to her dress and layers of strings on her wings, making sure both wings match.

2. Begin to add your tangles. We've gone for a square theme on the wings, with Keeko at the top, Bales in the middle, and Eye-wa at the bottom.

3. We've used Aztec for the top of the dress and Eke for the flowing skirt.

TANGLE KEY

Aztec: page 15
Bales: page 7
Eke: page 13
Eye-wa: page 12
Keeko: page 7
Printemps: page 9

4. Finish by filling in the **halo**. We shaded the halo and the top of the wings, too.

Halloween Pumpkin

You're in for a spooky treat this Halloween! Use a few Zentangle® tricks to craft this patterned pumpkin with slanted eyes and a ghoulish grin.

1. Draw or trace a simple pumpkin outline with curved lines coming from the stalk in the middle.

2. Choose a really bold tangle for the pumpkin itself. We've used Stricles. Start to draw in the eyes as well.

3. We used 'Nzeppel for the leaves and added short lines along the edge of the pumpkin stalk for shading.

TANGLE KEY

'Nzeppel : page 8
Stricles: page 14

4. Add some shading to the leaves, stalk, and mouth to finish your spooky pumpkin.

Easter Chick

Easter is a time for chicks, chocolate, and brightly painted eggs. Crack into your celebration with this newly hatched Zentangle® chick!

1. Draw the outline of two striped eggs and a chick hatching from a third egg.

2. Choose your tangles and start filling the spaces. We've used Cadent for the chick's head and body, Keeko for its wings, and Printemps for its chest.

3. We chose the same tangles for both of the unbroken eggs, alternating stripes of Chillon and Beeline.

TANGLE KEY

Beeline: page 16
Cadent: page 8
Chillon: page 17
Keeko: page 7
Printemps: page 9
Stoic: page 11

4. The chick's egg is filled with Stoic for an Easter basket effect.

Chinese Lantern

This Chinese lantern will bring light and fun to any party. We've mixed bold shapes and delicate patterns for a dramatic effect!

1. Start with the outline of a Chinese lantern. We've drawn strings across the lantern to split the space up, and to add extra detail to the top and bottom.

2. Now start to add tangles. We've used Aztec and Bales.

3. Keep filling the strings to build up the pattern. We've chosen Stricles for the top and bottom sections.

4. We've used Keeko and Eke for the hanging charm. Your ZIA is complete!

TANGLE KEY

Aztec: page 15
Bales: page 7
Eke: page 13
Keeko: page 7
Stricles: page 14

Glossary

3-D Stands for "3-dimensional." If a drawing or pattern looks 3-D, it looks like a solid object.

diagonal A straight line at an angle.

fairy lights A string of small lights, often used to decorate a Christmas tree.

grid A set of uniform squares made from straight lines or points

halo A disc above an angel's head.

horizontal A straight line that is parallel to the horizon, the imaginary line where the ground meets the sky.

pattern A set of shapes or a design that is repeated.

pine A type of evergreen tree with long, thin leaves known as needles.

texture The look or feel of a surface.

vertical A straight line running from top to bottom, or bottom to top.

woven A texture that looks as if it has been created by weaving.

Further Information

Books to Read

Holiday Crafts: 196 Crafts for Mother's Day, Father's Day, Valentine's Day, 4th of July, Halloween Crafts, Thanksgiving Crafts, & Christmas Crafts!
Kitty Moore
CreateSpace Independent Publishing Platform, 2015

Zentangle® for Kids
Jane Marbaix
Sterling Children's Books, 2015

Zentangle® for Kids: With Tangles, Templates, and Pages to Tangle On
Beate Winkler
Quarry Books, 2016

Websites

Visit Crayola's website for many printable holiday coloring pages.
http://www.crayola.com/free-coloring-pages/holidays/

Head over to this website for lots of Zentangle® coloring pages and other drawing tutorials.
http://www.supercoloring.com/coloring-pages/arts-culture/zentangle

Check out this website for Zentangle® coloring pages and lots of other activity ideas.
http://kidsactivitiesblog.com/?s=zentangle

Publisher's note to educators and parents: Our editors have carefully reviewed these websites to ensure that they are suitable for students. Many websites change frequently, however, and we cannot guarantee that a site's future contents will continue to meet our high standards of quality and educational value. Be advised that students should be closely supervised whenever they access the Internet.

Index